ATTENTION

SENIORS

BILL YEOMANS

Attention Seniors

Copyright © 2018 by William Yeomans

No part of this work may be copied or reproduced in any manner whatsoever, ether by print, or digital or electronic means or any other format or storage process without the express, written permission of the author.

This is a work of fictional humor. Any connection to real persons, living or dead, is purely a fictional coincidence. The entire content is derived only from the mind and experience of the author. No other sources were used.

LARGE PRINT EDITION

Cover Design: Cover Creator
ISBN: 13- 978-1723205972
ISBN: 10-1723205974

william.yeomans.fb@gmail.com

Books by this Author

<u>Power Verses</u> - To Strengthen Your Walk

<u>The Face of God</u> - Reflected in Nature

<u>Christ Centered Marriage</u>

<u>Christ Centered Finances</u>

<u>Christ Centered Families</u>

<u>Bill I Am</u> – An Autobiography

<u>My Heart Made New</u> A Personal Testimony

<u>Spirit Power</u> - Holy Spirit Throughout History

<u>Attention SENIORS</u> – Life's a Chuckle

Available on AMAZON

ABOUT THE AUTHOR

THIS BOOK IS WRITTEN

FOR SENIORS

BY A SENIOR

PASTOR BILL TURNED 80

THIS AUTHOR HAS

WALKED THE WALK

SO NOW HE CAN

TALK THE TALK

BECAUSE

AT TIMES

TALKING

IS MUCH EASIER

THAN WALKING!

LAUGHING FEELS REALLY GOOD

HOPE YOU CAN READ

THE 16 POINT PRINT!

Bill Yeomans

FORWARD

THIS IS A BOOK TO
BLESS YOUR SOUL
IT IS FILLED WITH HUMOR
GOOD, WHOLESOME HUMOR
TO MAKE THE HEART HAPPY
OLD FOLKS NEED TO CHUCKLE
ELSE OUR LIPS MAY CRACK
IT WILL MAKE YOU CHUCKLE
OR ASK YOUR MONEY BACK
GOOD LUCK WITH THAT
THERE IS A TABLE OF CONTENTS
THAT WAY
EVERY PAGE CAN BE
A NEW EXPERIENCE!
AND YOU WILL NEVER
LOSE YOUR DESTINY

Table of Contents

Books by this Author 3

ABOUT THE AUTHOR 4

FORWARD 5

VISION 15

ACHES AND PAINS 16

DIFFERENT COLORS 17

OCTOGENERIANS RULE! 19

ADMITTING THINGS 20

GOPHERS 21

NOAH 22

CHANGING WORDS 23

SENIORS LOSING IT 24

WESTERN MOVIES 25

SNAKES 26

CHICKENS 27

LITTLE THINGS	28
WORK	29
GOING	30
BEING FRIENDLY	31
SLOW	32
POWER	33
OLD PEOPLE	34
UP AND DOWN	35
LOSING THINGS	36
SKIN	37
THANKFULNESS	38
TONGUES	39
MORE ON TONGUES	41
MOVIE THEATERS	42
MORE OLD WESTERNS	43

STANDING AT ATTENTION 44

SPITTING 45

WEATHER 46

REACHING 47

PERFECTION 48

MORE PARTS 49

CHEWING GUM 50

SAVED FOR YOU 51

REMEMBER WHEN? 52

PUMPKINS 53

THE MANTLE CLOCK 54

TEMPER 55

WHY NOT? 56

CHANGE 2 57

BILLS 58

TREES	59
MUSHY	60
IS NOT - ARE NOT	61
SLEEPING	62
THE MOON	63
WAVES	64
SHIPS	65
RUSTY	66
SHARP	67
SHAKING	68
SHEARS	69
BALD AND GRAY	70
BANKS	71
THORNS	72
DOUBLES	73

TIME	74
PARTS	75
PARTING	76
POETRY	77
RELATIONS	78
STATEMENTS	79
CROOKED	80
WHISPERING	81
SERIOUS	82
LAUGHTER	83
WONDERING	84
TRAFFIC	85
TANKS	86
PASTOR TO PASTOR	87
CORN	88

BONES	89
CONNECTIONS	90
SMOKING	91
BIRDS	92
TEETH	93
LESSONS	94
WHISKERS	95
PUPPIES	96
RESTFUL	97
APRONS	98
SCRATCHING	99
CLOTHES LINES	100
CLOTHES LINES 2	101
PUDDLES	102
MEMORY	103

PAPERWORK 104

TEMPTATIONS 105

MENDING 106

LONELY 107

WONDERING 108

BUTTONS 109

VERTICAL 110

IN BETWEEN 111

PILL TAKERS 112

HALLS 113

SHIFTING 114

FOLLOWING 115

DREAMS 116

PROCRASTINATION 117

LIFTING 118

PERSONALITY	119
LAWYERS	120
FREEZING	121
MORE FREEZING	122
SOMEDAY – ONE DAY	123
GETTING SETTLED	124
LOSING IT	125
SCALES	126
STRETCHING	127
BENDING	128
WINDOWS	129
TIME TWO	130
SINGING	131
CLEANING	132
WORRY	133

ENDING 134

Books by this Author 135

Bill Yeomans

VISION

THERE ARE TWO TYPES OF VISION
ONE IS HELPED WITH GLASSES
OR A MAGNIFYING GLASS
MY FRIEND IS AT TIMES
LOSING HER GLASSES.
THEN SHE FINDS THEM
RIGHT WHERE SHE LEFT THEM
THEN SHE WIPES THEM CLEAN
THEY WON'T GET LOST AGAIN
FOR THE LIFE OF ME
I CAN'T REMEMBER WHAT
THE OTHER TYPE OF VISION IS!
ARE THERE REALLY TWO?
I THINK IT DEALS WITH FAITH
BETWEEN GOD AND YOU
NOT TUNNEL VISION

ACHES AND PAINS

A LITTLE OLD LADY
ONCE EXPLAINED
ARTHRITIS:
"AT MY AGE
IF IT DOESN'T HURT
IT DOESN'T WORK."

ANOTHER SENIOR STATED:
"ARTHUR IS MY
CONSTANT COMPANION.
WE WAKE UP TOGETHER
AND PAL AROUND ALL DAY"

"ARTHUR ONLY SLEEPS
WHEN I DO"

DIFFERENT COLORS

I AM AN OCTOGENARIAN.
IT'S A FACT!
I LOVE TO ENGAGE
WITH LITTLE CHILDREN.
IN A RESTAURANT
A 3-YEAR-OLD BOY
CAME UP TO ME
AND ASKED:
"WHY ARE YOUR TEETH
YELLOW?"
I TRIED IN VAIN TO EXPLAIN
HOW COFFEE OFTEN STAINS
HE LOOKED ME IN THE EYE
AND SAID:
"BOY ARE YOU OLD!"
I HAVE NEVER UNDERSTOOD

WHY WOMEN TRY TO HIDE
THE FACT THEIR HAIR
IS TURNING GREY
MEN, ON THE OTHER HAND
ARE WONDERING WHY
THEIR HAIR IS MOVING
FROM THEIR HEAD TO THE
EARS AND EYEBROWS.
WIGS AND TOUPE'S
MUST BE MAINLY MADE
FOR THOSE OF US WHO
ARE IN DEEP DENIAL
I'M NOT REALLY SURE
WHAT THAT MEANS.
IS DEEP DENIAL SERIOUS?
COULD YOU MAYBE DROWN?
MORE LIKE SOME CONDITION
CONDITIONER SOFTENS US

Bill Yeomans

OCTOGENERIANS RULE!

WE LIKE TO RULE
WE'RE REALLY GOOD AT IT
WE'VE BEEN DOING IT FOREVER
AND WE PLAN TO CONTINUE
IF WE CAN JUST REMEMBER HOW.
FIRST, START WITH A RULER
A WOODEN ONE WORKS BEST
RULERS ARE PRETTY HANDY
THEY CAN MEASURE RESULTS
EVEN USED TO RAP KNUCKLES
IN THE GOOD OLD DAYS
NOT ANY MORE, NO WAY-NO HOW
THINGS ARE A CHANGING
LADY RULERS RULE BETTER
HAVING MORE EXPERIENCE
BAKING PIES AND SUCH

ADMITTING THINGS

NO ONE LIKES TO ADMIT IT
THE WRINKLES TELL IT ALL
GRANDKIDS PAT US ON THE HEAD
AMUSED THAT WE'RE SO SMALL
I JUST REMEMBERED
THERE'S ANOTHER THING
RULERS ARE GOOD FOR…
….I JUST FORGOT!
RULERS ONLY WORK IN
ONE DIRECTION
MY FRIEND CANNOT DRIVE
WHILE BACKING UP.
SHE NEVER COULD
PERHAPS NEVER WILL
A SELF-DRIVING CAR?

GOPHERS

IN THE UNDERWORLD OF
GOPHERS, I MUST BE KING!
THEY CHOOSE MY LAWN FIRST
TO DO THEIR BURROWING.

WHILE SITTING IN MY GARDEN
NOT DOING A SINGLE THING
A GOPHER STUCK HER HEAD UP
AND BEGAN TO STARE AT ME
WE LOOKED EACH OTHER
IN THE EYE
FOR THE LIFE OF ME I
KNOW NOT WHY.
I THINK SHE TRIUMPHED
ONE GOPHER TO ANOTHER

NOAH

HERE WAS A REALLY OLD GUY
DIED AT AGE OF 950
HE WAS BORN AS A BABY
BEFORE HE GREW OLD
AT 600 HE ENTERED THE ARK
THE FIRST PETTING ZOO
FOLKS LIVED REALLY OLD
IN NOAH'S DAYS
BUT NOT ANYMORE
WERE THOSE FIRST CALLED
THE "GOOD OLD DAYS"?
DID NOAH GET 'TENNIS ELBOW'
FROM BUILDING THE ARK
NOBODY LEFT ALIVE
WHO REMEMBERS
OR EVEN WANTS TO

CHANGING WORDS

GRASS - SOMETHING TO MOW

HIGH FIVE - MORE THAN FOUR

LAME - NOT FUNNY

SUCK IT UP - BE STRONG

TWITTER - BIRD LANGUAGE

TWEETING - TWITTER TALK

A LEAKER - SECRET TALKER

CLOUD STORAGE - WORDS

RAIN STORAGE - CLOUDS

A HARD DRIVE - COMPUTERS

A STRAIGHT DRIVE - GOLF

A LEISURLY DRIVE - CAR

A LINE DRIVE - BASEBALL

A GREAT CATCH - BASEBALL

HOME RUN – RUNNING HOME

THE END - ENDING

SENIORS LOSING IT

SOME OF MY BEST FRIENDS
DON'T WRITE ANYMORE
THEY DON'T CALL ANYMORE
THEY CAN'T HEAR ANYMORE
THEY DON'T CARE ANYMORE
DON'T SWEAR ANYMORE
DON'T TEACH OTHERS TO SWEAR
SOME NEVER DID SWEAR
SOME USED TO SAY 'I SWEAR'
I DON'T THINK THAT COUNTS
SOME SWEAR ON THE BIBLE
EVEN ON THEIR MOTHERS GRAVE
MOSTLY IN THE OLD MOVIES
I SWEAR I REMEMBER THIS
I NEVER DID SWEAR MUCH
NOT THAT I REMEMBER - I SWEAR

Bill Yeomans

WESTERN MOVIES

YOU KNOW YOU'RE GETTING OLD
IF YOU REMEMBER:
WHEN ROY ROGERS AND
DALE EVANS GOT MARRIED
ROY'S HORSE WAS 'TRIGGER'
THE LONE RANGER
WAS SELDOM ALONE
HE HAD 'HI-HO SILVER-AWAY'
WHEREVER 'AWAY' WAS
HE ALSO HAD TONTO
WHO SAID 'KEMASABIE'
AND 'GETUM UP SCOUT'
THEY NEVER GOT MARRIED
NOT EVEN HAD GIRL FRIENDS
THEY WERN'T INVENTED YET
WAY BACK THEN

SNAKES

SNAKES MAKE GREAT PETS
WE CAPTURED METHODIST ONES
UNDER THE METHODIST STEPS
THEY LIVED FOR FREE
HIDING IN THE KITCHEN
TILL THEY FOUND MOTHER
SHE SET THEM FREE
GOPHER SNAKES EAT GOPHERS
RATTLE SNAKES RATTLE
SNAKES DON'T HAVE FEET
THEY HAVE NO LEGS, EITHER
THAT'S WHY THEY SLITHER
SATAN IS A SNAKE
KING SNAKES EAT KINGS
IN THE EARLY DAYS
THE DEVIL COULD WALK

Bill Yeomans

CHICKENS

CHICKENS HAVE NO TEETH
THAT'S WHY THE DON'T TALK
I WATCHED ONE LAY AN EGG
BOY DID SHE SQUAWK
CHICKENS DON'T HAVE LIPS
SO, THEY CAN'T WHISTLE
IF YOU BOIL AN EGG
IT BECOMES BOILED
IF TREATED VERY BADLY
IT BECOMES A DEVILED EGG
THEY SHOW UP AT EVERY
CHURCH PICNIC
TRYING TO GET SAVED
SADLY, ITS TOO LATE
FOR THE ONES GOT ATE
RIGHT OFF THE PLATE

LITTLE THINGS

GRANDMA TOLD ME THAT
LITTLE WHITE LIES
ARE NOT REALLY WHITE
WHY NOT CHANGE THEIR NAMES?
I WAS LITTLE ONE TIME
WHEN I SAT ON GRANDMAS LAP
WE WOULD ROCK AND ROCK
AND THEN I'D TAKE A NAP
ANTS ARE REALLY LITTLE
GOD GAVE THEM SIX LEGS
THREE ON EACH SIDE
HE MUST REALLY CARE
FOR ALL THE LITTLE THINGS
GRANDMA SAYS THAT LOVE
IS NO LITTLE THING
I THINK THAT SHE IS RIGHT

WORK

JUST SITTING IS HARD WORK
STANDING UP IS ALSO HARD
ESPECIALLY WHEN SITTING
WORK SUGGESTS MOTION
I GET MOTION SICKNESS
I GET SICK OF WORKING
I GET SICK AND TIRED
I THINK I'LL TAKE A NAP
NAPS ARE A FORM OF WORK
ESPECIALLY WHEN WAKING UP
REMEMBERING IS HARD WORK
FORGETTING IS EASY
NO PROBLEM AT ALL
I CAN DO THIS EVERY DAY
SEVERAL TIMES A DAY
I AM A NATURAL

GOING

GOING IS NOT COMING
IT'S DIFFERENT FROM COMING
IT'S HARD TO GET GOING
TO KNOW WHERE YOU'RE GOING
OR WHY YOU'RE GOING
OR EVEN CARE IF YOU'RE GOING
GOING INVOLVES GETTING UP
AND STANDING – LIKE GOING
MAYBE EVEN WALKING…
AND THEN YOUR GOUT
BEGINS TO SHOUT
YOU KNOW WHAT
I'M TALKING ABOUT
GOUT NEVER HAS HAD
A KIND THING TO TELL YOU
ALWAYS COMPLAINING

Bill Yeomans

BEING FRIENDLY

BEING FRIENDLY IS GOOD
IT PAYS BIG DIVIDENDS
MAKING A NEW FRIEND
IS AS GOOD AS CHOCOLATE?
FRIENDS TELL EACH OTHER
SECRETS
THEY LAUGH TOGETHER
THEY PLAY TOGETHER
THEY CRY TOGETHER
THEY PRAY TOGETHER
FRIENDS ARE GOOD FOR
EACH OTHER
FRIENDSHIP IS STILL FREE
NOBODY TAXES IT – EVER
A GOOD FRIEND
LASTS FOREVER

SLOW

SLOW IS OPPOSITE OF FAST
SLOW FEELS COMFORTABLE
A SLOWPOKE IS NOT A POKE
A POKE CAN BE PAINFUL
SLOW GIVES TIME TO THINK
AND TIME TO PLAN
AND TIME TO GET THINGS DONE
IF I CAN WALK SLOW
WHY CAN'T THE CLOCK
RUN SLOW?
LIFE IS A MYSTERY
ALL SLOWS ARE NOT EQUAL
MY SLOW IS NOT YOUR SLOW
MINE IS BETTER
BECAUSE IT'S SLOWER
MY SLOW IS SO SLOW…

Bill Yeomans

POWER

POWER COMES IN MANY SIZES
A LITTLE TINY BUTTON
MOVES CAR WINDOWS UP
AND THEN IT MOVES THEM DOWN
POWER GIVES US CONTROL
SOMETIMES I LOSE CONTROL
OF ALMOST EVERYTHING
I KNOW WHAT YOU'RE THINKING
NO, I DON'T!
USE POWER CAREFULLY
AND YOU DON'T GET SHOCKED
GOD HAS GREAT POWER
HE CREATED ADAM
OUT OF DIRT
THEN HE CREATED A FLOWER
IS THAT 'FLOWER POWER'?

OLD PEOPLE

WHEN I START TO PONDER
MY MIND BEGINS TO WANDER
WHERE IT GOES, NOBODY KNOWS
OLD PEOPLE ARE EITHER
GRUMPY OR KIND
I THINK KIND IS BETTER
OLD PEOPLE ARE SOFTER
YOUNG ONES MOVE TOO FAST
TRYING TO GET OLD
OLD HAPPENS ALL BY ITSELF
IT DOESN'T NEED ANY HELP
IT JUST APPEARS
IT'S THERE
BEFORE WE EVEN KNOW IT
OLD AGE IS HARD TO RECOGNIZE
UNLESS YOU HAVE A MIRROR

Bill Yeomans

UP AND DOWN

UP AND DOWN ARE DIFFERENT
THEY ARE SPELLED DIFFERENT
THEY EVEN LOOK DIFFERENT
UP IS UP AND DOWN IS DOWN
IT'S REALLY NOT THAT HARD
YOU NEED TO TRY IT
GETTING UP IS HARDER
THAN SITTING DOWN
LAYING DOWN IS BETTER
THAN FALLING DOWN
FALLING DOWN HURTS
FOR DAYS AND DAYS AND DAYS
SITTING DOWN ONLY HURTS
WHEN YOU SIT TOO LONG
UP AND DOWN MAKES ME TIRED
JUST THINKING MAKES ME TIRED

LOSING THINGS

LOSING STUFF IS AN ADVENTURE
SOMETIME IT FINDS ITSELF
USUALLY WHERE YOU LEFT IT
FINDING IS BETTER THAN LOSING
I HAVE LOST MY WAY
I HAVE LOST MY APPETITE
I HAVE LOST DIRECTION BUT
I'VE NEVER LOST MY MIND
AFTER READING THIS BOOK
YOU MAY DISAGREE. SOME PANIC
WHEN THEY LOSE STUFF
CELL PHONES TOP THE LIST
ALL THEIR FRIENDS ARE HIDING
IN ONE TINY DISK
OUR PHONES HAD CORDS
YOU NEVER LOST THEM

Bill Yeomans

SKIN

YOUR SKIN IS AN ORGAN
A REALLY OLD ORGAN
LIKE THE CHURCH PUMP ORGAN
HOW DEEP IS SKIN DEEP?
WHY DOES YOUR SKIN CRAWL?
YOUR BIGGEST ORGAN OF ALL
SHOULD LEARN TO WALK
CRAWLING IS FOR BABIES
YOUR SKIN IS WAY TOO OLD
OLD SKIN COVERS OLD PEOPLE
TO KEEP THEM WARM
THE WRINKLES TRAP WARM AIR
WRINKLES HIDE THE SCARS
EVEN DEEP SCARS
GOD UNDERSTOOD
HE MADE WRINKLES

THANKFULNESS

GRANDMA SAID BE THANKFUL
FOR EVERY LITTLE THING
WHAT ABOUT THE BIG THINGS?
THANK HIM IN THE MORNING
WHEN YOU WAKE UP
BECAUSE YOU CAN GET UP
BE THANKFUL YOU HAVE TEETH
TEETH HELP YOU CHEW
SOME COME OUT AT NIGHT
BE THANKFUL FOR THEM TOO
BE CAREFUL NOT TO LOSE THEM
WHEN THEY COME OUT AT NIGHT
LIKE THE STARS
BE THANKFUL WE CAN SEE STARS
THEY TELL US
HOW SMALL WE ARE

Bill Yeomans

<u>TONGUES</u>

TONGUES ARE VERY TINY
PEOPLE SPEAK IN TONGUES
THEY CAN CURSE WITH TONGUES
DOGS KISS WITH TONGUES
PEOPLE LICK WITH TONGUES
I'M THINKING OF ICE CREAM
TONGUES CAN WAGGLE
TONGUES ARE EVEN SHARP
THEY CAN BE HURTFUL
WHEN THEY ARE EXTRA SHARP
NOT LIKE WITH CHEESE
WHEN EXTRA SHARP IS GOOD
TONGUES CAN BE FORKED
WHEN THEY WAG BOTH WAYS
USE OUR TONGUES FOR GOOD
GIVING GOD THE PRAISE

Attention Seniors

USE THIS PAGE TO REST A BIT

Bill Yeomans

MORE ON TONGUES

TONGUES CAN BE WAGGING
LIKE PUPPY DOG TAILS
WHAT DOES IT MEAN
TO BITE YOUR TONGUE?
DOESN'T THIS HURT?
WHY IS THIS IMPORTANT?
ONE BIG MYSTERY
TONGUES CAN BE UPLIFTING
STRONG AS THEY CAN BE
HAVING LOTS OF POWER
WHEN USED QUITE LOVINGLY
NEVER STICK OUT YOUR TONGUE
EXCEPT TO CATCH A FLY
OR A SNOWFLAKE
OR TO TOUCH YOUR NOSE
IF YOU'RE ONE OF THOSE

MOVIE THEATERS

ARE PLACES WE USED TO GO
TO WATCH MOVIES
AND EAT POPCORN
AND CHEW CHEWING GUM
AND DEPOSIT THE STALE WAD
UNDER THE THEATER SEAT
TO MARK YOUR FAVORITE SPOT
FOR NEXT WEEK
THEY STARTED WITH SILENT FILM
THE ONES WITHOUT SOUND
YOU COULDN'T HEAR THEM
THEN TALKING PICTURES CAME
YOU REMEMBER WHEN
YOU WERE THERE, THEN
PICTURES STARTED TALKING
HOW AMAZING!

Bill Yeomans

MORE OLD WESTERNS

YOU ARE REALLY OLD
IF YOU REMEMBER
'GABBY HAYES'
HE TALKED TO HIS HORSE
"OK PAINT, LET'S GET
WHERE WE AINT"
YOU DO REMEMBER GABBY
HE PLAYED WITH
'HOPALONG CASSIDY'
NOW THAT'S A NAME TO
REMEMBER, BUT I DON'T KNOW
WHERE HE HOPPED ALONG TO
HIS LADY FRIEND WAS
'NEVADA JANE'
YOU MUST REMEMBER JANE
EVERYONE REMEMBERS JANE

STANDING AT ATTENTION

WHEN STANDING AT ATTENTION
BACK STRAIGHT, KNEES LOCKED
WHAT KIND OF A LOCK?
EYES FACING FORWARD
WHO HAS BACKWARD EYES?
TEACHER SAYS "PAY ATTENTION"
WHY DO WE HAVE TO PAY?
HOW MUCH DO I NEED TO PAY?
DO I NEED REAL MONEY?
WILL MONOPLY MONEY DO?
I FOUND SOME UNDER THE BED
DIDN'T OTHER PEOPLE PAY?
IF YOU PAY CLOSE ATTENTION
THAT MUST COST MORE.
ATTENTION IS NEVER FREE
HOW CLOSE IS CLOSE TO YOU?

SPITTING

I'M TOLD OLD GRANNY
USED TO CHEW
JUST A TINY BIT
TO MAKE ENOUGH SALIVA
THEN SHE HAD TO SPIT
GRANNY TRIED TO PRACTICE
WHEN NOBODY WAS AROUND
EXCEPT A HAPLESS COCKROACH
THAT GRANNY TRIED TO DROWN
SPITOONS WERE PUT IN PLACES
WHERE LADIES SHOULDN'T GO
MADE OF SHINY POLISHED BRASS
SPITTING TAKES GREAT PRACTICE
OR YOU MIGHT DROOL INSTEAD
DROOLING IS FOR OLD FOLKS
TRY NOT TO SPIT IN BED

WEATHER

ALL SENIORS KNOW
ALL ABOUT THE WEATHER
WE CAN FEEL IT IN OUR BONES
FROM OUR NOSE TO OUR TOES
TOO COLD, THEN TOO HOT
WE CAN'T FIND A PERFECT SPOT
FIRE KEEPS US WARM
IT ALWAYS HAS
AS LONG AS I REMEMBER
WHICH MAY NOT BE LONG AT ALL
COLD WEATHER IS THE COLDEST
WE ALL SEEM TO AGREE
SENIORS START TO SHIVER
WHEN IT GETS TO EIGHTY-THREE
THEN THE SUMMER COMES
REMIND ME, WHAT IS SUMMER?

Bill Yeomans

REACHING

REACHING UP HIGH IS
JUST LIKE BASKETBALL
NO GOOD UNLESS YOU'RE TALL
REACHING YOUR POTENTIAL
IS FINDING YOUR TOOTHBRUSH
OR BENDING DOWN
TO TIE YOUR SHOES
REACHING IS STREACHING
TWO KINDS OF PAIN
A PAIN IN THE NECK
OR IN THE BEHIND
REACHING BACK IN TIME
IS A BIT LIKE JOGGING?
ALL OF THIS REACHING
IS JUGGLING MY MIND
ARE WE THERE YET?

PERFECTION

PERFECTION IS NOT REJECTION
PERFECTION IS A TEST
FOR DOING YOUR VERY BEST
NEVER WAS A PERFECT MAN
JUST THAT ONE - YOU KNOW WHO
I'M TALKING ABOUT
HIS 'DADDY' IS PERFECT, TOO
NOT LIKE ME & NOT LIKE YOU
PERFCT ESCAPES ME EVERY DAY
A GOOD CUP OF COFFEE
IS ALMOST PERFECT
A GOOD BACK RUB WORKS
A NAP WITHOUT INTERRUPTION
THE LACK OF HURTING PARTS
NOT LOSING ANY PARTS
OR FINDING EXTRA PARTS

Bill Yeomans

MORE PARTS

AUTO PARTS ARE NOT
PEOPLE PARTS, HOWEVER
THEY BOTH CAN WEAR OUT
THE BEST PART OF A BOOK
IS OFTEN THE LAST PAGE?
SIMILAR TO SOME OLD FOLKS
GIVING AN ORGAN RECITAL
USUALLY OFF KEY
LIKE A SCREECHING VIOLIN
NOT PLEASANT TO THE EARS.
WHO CARES ABOUT ORGANS?
ONES THEY MAY HAVE LOST
OR HAD REMOVED
THIS IS SO SAD
ALL BODY PARTS WEAR OUT
SOME WAY TOO FAST

CHEWING GUM

ALL GUM IS NOT EQUAL
IN THE VERY GOOD OLD DAYS
GUM CAME IN LITTLE SQUARES
TWELVE TO A BOX-TWO FLAVORS
SPEARMINT AND PEPPERMENT
ALL THAT GUM WAS 'MINTY'
IT WORKED RATHER WELL
TO KEEP THE BREATH FRESH
JUST IN CASE
I NEVER BOUGHT IT BY THE CASE
TOO MUCH TO SPEND FOR GUM
WE USED TO CHEW UNTIL
ALL THE 'MINTY' WAS GONE
OR, OUR JAWS GOT TIRED
OR WE SPIT IT OUT
NOT LIKE TOBACCO CHEW

Bill Yeomans

SAVED FOR YOU

THIS IS YOUR PAGE TO WRITE

YOUR OWN LIMERICK OR RHYME

REMEMBER WHEN?

FORTY MEANT 'OLDER PERSON'
HAIR COLOR WAS NATURAL
CRUSING WAS DONE IN BOATS
A LEAKER LEFT A PUDDLE
INSTANT MEALS WERE RAW
LADIES WERE LADIES
EXCEPT AT BARGAIN SALES
MEN WERE STILL GENTLEMEN
LEADERS ACTUALLY LED
FAMLIES ATE TOGETHER
TELEPHONES HAD CORDS
WITH PARTY LINES
WITH OTHERS LISTENING IN
OPERATORS "NUMBER PLEASE"
WITH ALL PHONES CONNECTED
TO SOME WALL

Bill Yeomans

PUMPKINS

PUMPKINS GROW IN DIRT
THEY GROW ON PUMPKIN VINES
WITH SMILES ON THEIR FACES
AND SEEDS IN THEIR TUMMIES
LOTS AND LOTS OF SEEDS.
BIBLES SAY TO SPREAD SEEDS
ARE THESE ANY OLD SEEDS?
OR VERY SPECIAL SEEDS
LIKE PUMPKINS MAKE
PUMPKINS MAKE KIDS HAPPY
BY GIVING ALL THEY GOT
KIDS WILL CUT THEM OPEN
ADULTS CLEAN OUT 'GUK'
SOME DRY OUT THE SEEDS
FOR PLANTING IN THE SPRING
GOD GIVES LIFE TO EVERYTHING

THE MANTLE CLOCK

OUR MANTLE CLOCK REMEMBERS
TIMES WHEN TIME STOOD STILL
WHEN THE OLD WIND UP SPRING
HAD GIVEN ALL SHE GOT, AND
ELECTRIC CLOCKS WERE NOT
MANTLE CLOCK KEPT TICKING
AS LONG AS SHE GOT CARE
WHEN OUR CLOCK WAS TICKING
THERE WAS NO DESPAIR
MANTLE CLOCK WOULD LISTEN
TO EVERY SPOKEN WORD
SOME WERE GOOD, SOME NOT
GOD IS SOMETIMES SIMILAR
TO OUR OLD MANTLE CLOCK
HE HEARS OUR EVERY WORD
SOME GOOD – SOME NOT

TEMPER

TEMPER IS ELUSIVE
IT SELDOM MEANS THE SAME
STEEL CAN BE TEMPERED WITH A
HOT AND CONSTANT FLAME
STEEL, WHEN IT IS TEMPERED
TAKES THE 'TEMPERED' NAME
AND THAT IS A GOOD THING
IT MAKES THE STEEL STRONGER
USEFUL FOR MORE THINGS
SOME FOLKS GET OLDER AND
TEND TO LOSE THEIR TEMPER
THIS IS NOT A GOOD THING
IT'S HARD TO FIND AGAIN
SO, KEEP YOUR TEMPER CLOSE
NEVER SET IT FREE, AND THEN
KEEP YOUR FRIENDS HAPPY

WHY NOT?

MY INITIALS ASK A QUESTION
THEY ASK THE QUESTION, <u>WHY</u>?
I ASK ANOTHER QUESTION
"WHY NOT"? IS MY REPLY
GIVE AWAY A DOZEN SMILES
ADD A HUG OR TWO
TELL SOMEONE YOU LOVE THEM
AND SHOW YOU MEAN IT TOO
LOOK OUT TO BE HELPFUL
LOOK IN FOR INNER STRENGTH
YOU CANNOT OUTGIVE THE LORD
YOU WERE BORN BUTT NAKED
NOW THAT'S A PICTURE
NOT AS WRINKLED THEN
OLD AGE IS A BLESSING
WE'VE SO MUCH MORE TO GIVE

CHANGE 2

NO MATTER - CHANGE HAPPENS
CHANGE CONTROLS THINGS
IT HAPPENS – WE GET OLDER
WE CAN MAKE CHANGE
IF WE CAN COUNT, AND SEE
AND MOSTLY CAN THINK
AND USUALLY REMEMBER
IT MAKES HOLES IN POCKETS
AND WEIGHS DOWN YOUR PURSE
THIS CREATES HIP PROBLEMS
AND OFTEN BACK PROBLEMS
IT BECOMES A PAIN IN THE NECK
CHANGE CAN BE TROUBLING
LIKE A MOTHER-IN-LAW
YOU COULD JUST ROLL HER UP
AND TAKE HER TO THE BANK

BILLS

THERE ARE TWO KINDS OF BILLS
THE FRIENDLY GREEN KIND
AND THE PESKY UNPAID KIND
I LIKE THE GREEN KIND BETTER
THERE'S ONLY ONE BIG PROBLEM
GREEN BILLS NEVER HANG OUT
ALWAYS SOMEWHERE TO GO
ONCE GONE THEY STAY GONE
NOT LIKE THE UNPAID KIND
THEY INVITE THEIR FRIENDS
AND COUSINS TWICE REMOVED
YOU CAN'T PAY THEM TO LEAVE
THESE RELATIVES SOON RETURN
GETTING BIGGER AND BIGGER
I WONDER IF THEY WILL BUST
THEY SEEM TO KEEP ME BUSTED

Bill Yeomans

TREES

TREES GIVE MOST EVERYTHING
A PLACE FOR BIRDS TO SING
AND TO BUILD THEIR HOMES
TO RAISE THEIR BIRDIE BABIES
TREES ARE LIKE GREAT PERSONS
WITH NOTHING GREAT TO PROVE
THEY LET YOU KNOW THEIR AGE
BY COUNTING EVERY GROOVE
REDWOODS IN CALIFORNIA
TELL WHEN COLUMBUS SAILED
OLD OLIVE TREES IN ISRAEL
GAVE THE SAVIOR SHADE
CEDAR TREES BECAME AN ARK
GOD PLANTED THE FIRST TREES
HIS SON DIED ON A TREE AS WELL

MUSHY

SOMETIMES I GET MUSHY
LIKE AN OLD APPLE
MUSHY APPLES ONLY GO
TWO WAYS, SO I THINK,
INTO SLOPPY APPLESAUCE
OR APPLE CIDER DRINK
A CONSTANT STATE OF MUSHY
IS NOT A PLACE TO BE
BECAUSE A MUSHY ANYTHING
WILL DROP RIGHT OFF IT'S TREE
A LITTLE BIT OF MUSHY
GOES A LONG, LONG WAY
AS YOU GO THROUGH LIFE
REMEMBER
MUSHY APPLES ATTRACT WORMS
STAND FIRM, OLD FRIENDS

Bill Yeomans

IS NOT - ARE NOT

A HOLE IN ONE IS NOT

A HOLY ONE

MADE IN CHINA IS NOT

FINE CHINA

PLEXIGLASS IS NOT

TEMPERED GLASS

OREOS ARE NOT

HEALTH FOOD

DANDYLIONS ARE NOT

HUNGRY LIONS

MUSCLE BOUND IS NOT

HOMEWARD BOUND

A WISE CRACKER IS NOT

A FIRE CRACKER

A BULL DOG IS NOT

A HOT DOG

SLEEPING

SLEEPING IS DIFFERENT FROM
NAPPING BY A LITTLE BIT
BOTH ARE COMFORT ZONES
I ZONE WHILE SLEEPING
THAT'S A DIFFERENT TIME ZONE
WAKING UP BOTHERS ME SOME
CAN'T TELL WHERE I AM
OR EVEN IF I AM
OR WHERE I'VE BEEN
NOT KNOWING IS NEVER GOOD
I'M TOLD I SNORE REAL GOOD
WE ALL NEED SOMETHING SMALL
THAT WE EXCEL AT
WITH ME IT IS SLEEPING
I SLEEP SUPER GOOD
NAPPING IS A SPECIAL GIFT

Bill Yeomans

THE MOON

THE MOON IS NOT GREEN CHEESE
THE MAN IN THE MOON LEFT
HE CAME BACK TO EARTH
WITH HIS FRIEND AND ROCKS
WHAT IS A LOVERS MOON?
I'V HEARD TELL OF MOONSHINE
I'V SEEN MOONBEAMS SHINE
WHEN THE SUN IS SLEEPING
DOES THE MOON SLEEP TOO?
DOES THE MOON LIKE STARS?
WE GET SUNBURN
WHEN DO WE GET MOONBURN?
WHAT DOES IT MEAN
TO BE MOONSTRUCK?
WOULD THE MOON DO THAT?
CAN THE MOON MAKE WAVES?

WAVES

I OVERHEARD GRANDMA SAY
"NOW, LET'S NOT MAKE WAVES"
CAN PEOPLE DO THAT?
THAT JOB IS THE MOON'S
CAN PEOPLE STEAL HIS JOB?
WE SHOULDN'T MAKE WAVES
DON'T SADDEN THE MOON
THAT IS NEVER A GOOD IDEA
WAVES GROW IN OCEANS
AND CRASH ON THE ROCKS
EVEN WEAR DOWN ROCKS
WAVES ARE SO COOL
THEY NEVER GIVE UP
BREAKING ROCKS ALL DAY
I WANT TO BE LIKE A WAVE

SHIPS

SHIPS ARE LIKE BOATS
ONLY MUCH BIGGER
SHIPS RIDE THE OCEAN WAVES
SAILORS REALLY LOVE WAVES
BLONDS AND REDHEADS MOSTLY
SOME SHIPS DISPLAY SAILS
FILLED UP WITH WIND, BLOWING
SOME OLD MEN DO THE SAME
SOME ARE OLD WINDBAGS
SEVERAL WAYS TO BLOW WIND
GENTLEMEN BLOW THEIR NOSES
UNGENTLEMEN BLOW OFF STEAM
OLD FOLKS EVEN BREAK WIND
BUT DO IT SILENTLY
DOES WIND STAY BROKEN?

RUSTY

I HAD A RUSTY LOOKING DOG
WE EVEN CALLED HIM 'RUSTY'
SOMETIMES NAILS GET RUSTY
NEVER YOUR FINGERNAILS
THEY DO AT TIMES GET DIRTY
OXYGEN WITH WATER MIXED
TOGETHER CAUSES RUSTY
OLDER MEN NEED OXYGEN
IT HELPS TO CATCH OUR BREATH
CAN BREATH RUN AWAY?
LIKE RUSTY CHASING RABBITS
AT TIMES I THINK DEEPLY
LIKE BEFORE I TAKE A NAP
I NEED TO KNOW BEFORE I SLEEP
WHEN I'M RESTING
AM I RUSTING?

Bill Yeomans

SHARP

SHARP IS NOT DULL, UNLESS
IT LOSES BEING SHARP
SORT OF LIKE SOME PEOPLE
STEEL SHARPENS STEEL, OLD
PEOPLE NEED TO STAY SHARP
DULL DOESN'T WORK TOO WELL
WORKING MAKES YOU SHARP
DON'T CUT OFF YOUR NOSE
TO SPITE YOUR FACE
A CUT NOSE IS REALLY GROSS
NEVER PICK YOUR NOSE
AT LEAST NOT IN PUBLIC
WHEN PEOPLE SEE YOU DO IT
YOU WOULD NOT LOOK SHARP
YOU REMEMBER 'GILLETT'
LOOK SHARP, FEEL SHARP

SHAKING

SHAKING IS REALLY AN ART
OLDER FOLKS DO IT BEST
'SHAKE A LEG' SOME WOULD SAY
WHY SHAKE ONLY ONE LEG?
SOME OF US ONLY HAVE ONE LEG
THAT'S ME – HOW ABOUT YOU?
PEPPER SHAKERS CHALLENGE
THE VERY BEST OF SHAKERS
SHAKE OFF CRITICISM
LEARN TO SHAKE WITH JOY
WHEN TEMPTATION TEMPTS YOU
PRACTICE SHAKING? "NO"
SHAKING SAYS I'M GETTING OLD
MAYBE EVEN GETTING COLD
SHAKE FOR JOY WHILE YOU CAN
LEARN TO BE A HAPPY MAN

Bill Yeomans

SHEARS

SHEARS ARE BUILT FOR CUTTING
I BET YOU KNOW THAT
WHAT ABOUT PINKING SHEARS?
DO THEY CUT ONLY PINK STUFF?
THAT SOUNDS RIGHT TO ME
GRASS SHEARS CUT THE GRASS
BUT NOT BY THEMSELVES
SOMEONE NEEDS TO WORK THEM
SCISSORS ARE BABY SHEARS
THEY DO THE EASY JOBS
LIKE CUTTING TOENAILS
OR TRIMMING YOUR MUSTASH
OR PERFORMING A HAIRCUT
WHEN SCISSORS GROW OLD
THEY TURN INTO SHEARS

BALD AND GRAY

MELATIN MAKES HAIR GRAY
WHEN THEY TAKE IT AWAY
SOME SCIENTISTS SAY.
BUT GETTING BALD IS DIFFERENT
IN EVERY SINGLE WAY
BALD MEN LOOK FOR SINGLE
HAIRS TO REMOVE BALDING
WOMEN LOVE BALD MEN
SOMETHING TO KEEP SHINING
SAVING MONEY ON SHAMPOO
ANY WASHCLOTH WILL DO
GRAY EVEN SOUNDS OLD
IT MAKES YOU FEEL OLD
BALD HEADS SHINE THROUGH
ALL THE GRAY AND GLOOM
BALD LIGHTS UP ANY ROOM

Bill Yeomans

BANKS

SOME BANKS HAVE FOUR LEGS
AND LITTLY PIGGY FACES
TO HIDE THE DIMES AND DOLARS
IN YOUR SECRET PLACES.
NEVER BREAK A PIGGY BANK
ITS SURE TO BRING BAD LUCK
OLDER BANKS WERE DIFFERENT
LOOKED AT YOU THROUGH BARS
THEY COULD NOT GET OUT?
ONE DAY THE BARS GOT GONE
THEY RAN FAR AWAY
GRANNY KEEPS HER MONEY
IN A JAR HIGH ON THE SHELF
NEVER HAD A PIGGY BANK
GUESS SHE JUST LOST OUT

THORNS

THORNS ARE NOT STICKERS
BUT THEY BOTH HAVE PRICKERS
MOST ROSES HAVE THORNS
FOUND MOSTLY ON THE STEM
ROSE THORNS MAKE YOU BLEED
WE CONSIDER THORNY ISSUES
AND WEIGH THEM CAREFULLY
ARE BLEEDING HEARTS
THE SAME AS BROKEN HEARTS
THORNS SEEM COMPLICATED
HARD TO FIGURE OUT
BIG ONES PROTECT RASBERRIES
THEY HIDE UNDER LEAVES
WAITING FOR YOUR FINGERS
JUST TO MAKE YOU SHOUT

Bill Yeomans

DOUBLES

DOUBLES GO TOGETHER
ARE MORE THAN SINGLES
DOUBLE - PLY WORKS BEST
DOUBLE SAVES MANY PROBLEMS
DOUBLE PORTIONS ARE GOOD
DOUBLE TROUBLE NOT SO MUCH
DOUBLE VISION IS NO FUN
SEEING TWO OF EVERYTHING
WHEN THERE IS ONLY ONE
TWINS COUNT AS DOUBLES
SINCE THEY COME IN TWO'S
DOUBLE UP A MOORING LINE
TO KEEP YOUR SHIP SECURE
DOUBLE THE PLEASURE
DOUBLE THE FUN, WITH
DOUBLEMINT GUM

TIME

I WATCHED THE SANDS OF TIME
RUN THROUGH THE HOUR GLASS
EACH TINY GRANULE CHOSEN
FOR PERFECT WEIGHT AND SIZE
TO REPRESENT OUR PASSING
YOUR HOURS AND MINE
OUR TIME IS SO PRECIOUS
WE CAN NEVER GET IT BACK
WHEN GONE ITS GONE FOREVER
MY TIME IS SO ILLUSIVE
SLIPPING BY ON ME
I NEVER KNEW HOW SLIPPERY
TIL TURNING EIGHTY
EIGHTY ISN'T TERRIBLY OLD
JUST A LOT OF SEASONING

Bill Yeomans

PARTS

DIFFEENT PARTS ARE NEEDED
BEFORE WE HAVE THE WHOLE
WE HAVE AUTO PARTS STORES
WHY NOT HUMAN PARTS?
JUST BUY THEM OFF THE SHELF
GREASE THEM UP REAL WELL
AND THEN WE'RE GOOD TO GO
BOVINE TENDONS FROM A COW
PIG VALVES IN THE HEART
MAYBE SOMEDAY LAME-BRAINS
WHERE DO 'LAMES' COME FROM?
MY SURGEON TOOK MY LEG VEIN
AND ATTACHED IT TO MY HEART
THEN MY <u>OLD</u> LEG VEIN
GAVE ME A <u>NEW</u> START
OLD IS BEAUTIFUL!

PARTING

PARTING HAS MIXED RESULTS
SOME WOMEN PART THEIR HAIR
MOSES PARTED THE RED SEA
AND OLD AS I'VE GROWN TO BE
I REALLY WASN'T THERE
GOOD BOOK SAYS IT HAPPENED
THAT'S GOOD ENOUGH FOR ME
WHEN I THINK OF PARTING
SOMETIMES IT MAKES ME SAD
THE PROMISED REUNITING
TURNS ALL SAD TO GLAD
PARTING NEVER SAYS GOOD-BYE
JUST I'LL SEE YOU IN THE SKY
BABIES KNOW TO WAVE BYE-BYE
SO MUST YOU - SO MUST I

Bill Yeomans

POETRY

A POEM OFTEN MELTS A HEART
LIKE CHOCOLATE IN THE SUN
THINGS AT TIMES GET 'GUSHY'
BEFORE THE POEM IS DONE
A COWARD WILL NOT A POET BE
ONLY HEROS LIKE YOU AND ME
FAINT HEARTS WILL NOT
WRITE POETRY
POETS OPEN UP THEIR HEART
WORDS SPILL FROM THE START
POETIC WORDS BRING PLEASURE
WHEREVER THEY ABOUND
BRING TEARS OF ABJECT JOY
WHENEVER THEY ARE FOUND
POETS DIE OF OLD AGE
POEMS NEVER DO

RELATIONS

RELATIONS ARE NOT ALWAYS
RELATED TO EACH OTHER
RELATIONSHIPS CAN BE LEAKY
LIKE SHIPS FULL OF HOLES
SAME ROOT WORD AS RELATIVE
CAN'T CHOOSE 'EM OR LOSE 'EM
AT TIMES CAN'T STAND THEM
LIKE A DESSERT CACTUS
DRY AND FULL OF 'PRICKLES'
SOME RELATION-SHIPS SINK
OR SLOWLY FLOAT AWAY
RELATIONS ARE NOT ONLY SAD
SOME ARE FILLED WITH GLEE
JUST LIKE ALL MY RELATIVES
SINCE THEY EACH LOVE ME

Bill Yeomans

STATEMENTS

DIFFERENT FROM BREATH MINTS
AT TIMES I LOSE MY BREATH
MIND YOU, NOT OUT OF BREATH
SOMETIMES JUST CAN'T FIND IT
RETIREMENT IS WHEN
FREE TIME STANDS STILL
STATEMENTS ASKING MONEY
NEVER OPEN THAT KIND
THER'RE JUST A WASTE OF TIME
ARRIVE WITH POSTAGE DUE
YOU CAN RETURN TO SENDER
MAYBE THEY GOT LOST
OR TORN TO LITTLE SHREDS
STATEMENTS ARE QUESTIONS
WITH EXCLAMATION MARKS

CROOKED

GRANDMA'S CANE WAS CROOKED
IT STILL REACHED THE GROUND
CROOKED BUILDS CHARACTER
IT STABILIZED GRANDMA'S GAIT
SHE DIDN'T WOBBLE ANY MORE
SHE TOOK THAT CROOKED CANE
EVERY PLACE SHE WENT
MOSES HAD A CROOKED STAFF
MOST POWERFUL TO SEE
IT ATE UP PHAROAH'S SERPENT
GOD'S PEOPLE CROSSED THE SEA
GRANDMA HAD A CROOKED CANE
OLD MOSES HELD A STAFF
CROOKED DID NOT DEFINE HIM
HE WALKED A GODLY PATH

WHISPERING

WHISPERS ARE TALKING SOFTLY
THEY HELP PEOPLE LISTEN
THEY ENCOURAGE CLOSENESS
TREES WHISPER IN THE BREEZE
OTHER TREES WILL UNDERSTAND
WHISPERS BEAT SHOUTED WORDS
THEY ARE FILLED WITH PEACE
WHISPERS CARRY SECRETS
NEVER THE NAUGHTY KIND
IF SOMEONE HOLLERS INSULTS
A WHISPER BLOWS THEIR MIND
A WHISPER HOLDS REAL POWER
IT REACHES GOD ABOVE
HE ANSWERS WITH A WHISPER
HE'S A GOD OF LOVE

SERIOUS

GRANDMA SAID "GET SERIOUS"
WHERE DO YOU FIND IT?
DID IT GET LOST SOMEWHERE?
PERHAPS SERIOUS IS HIDING OUT
WAITING FOR ME TO LEAVE
I DON'T EVEN KNOW SERIOUS
WILL I RECOGNIZE IT, IF I SEE IT?
I GET CONFUSED SOMETIMES
DO YOU KNOW SERIOUS?
WILL YOU INTRODUCE HER TO ME
CAN I SEND FOR HER ON AMAZON
CHECK HER OUT ON GOOGLE
SERIOUS IS GOOD AT HIDING
SHE IS REALLY, REALLY, GOOD
I'M NOT TOO GOOD AT FINDING
SERIOUS IS STAYING LOST

Bill Yeomans

LAUGHTER

HAVE YOU HEARD A FUNNY
STORY OR MAYBE A GOOD JOKE
LIFE IS JUST TOO SERIOUS,
WORLD NEEDS TO LAUGH A BIT
TO 'TWIDDLE' A LITTLE BIT
WHAT IS A 'TWIDDLE'?
I THINK MAYBE A TINY LAUGH
MAYBE A TEENAGE CHUCKLE
MAYBE A NERVOUS MOTION
EMULATING GLEE, OR HAPPY
HAVE YOU HEARD OF
'TWIDDLD DEE - DEE'?
I THOUGHT OF THAT JUST NOW
IT JUST SEEMED TO COME
ESPECIALLY TO ME
LAUGH IF YOU AGREE

WONDERING

I WAS WONDERING
LOTS OF THINGS I DO NOT KNOW
WHY DID CURIOSITY KILL A CAT?
AND WHY WOULD SATISFACTION
WANT TO BRING IT BACK?
DON'T DEAD CATS SMELL BAD?
WHO WAS SATISFACTION?
DID YOU EVER MEET HER?
HAVE YOU EVEN SEEN HER?
DOES SHE REALLY EXIST? WHO
WOULD PICK UP A DEAD CAT?
ARE WE GETTING ANY ANSWERS?
QUESTIONS NEVER SATISFY
WITHOUT REAL GOOD ANSWERS
WHERE ARE THE ANSWERS?
HIDING IN THE CLOUDS?

Bill Yeomans

TRAFFIC

TRAFFIC SELDOM HAPPENED
TILL THEY INVENTED CARS
WHY ARE BUNCHED UP AUTOS
CALLED A TRAFFIC JAM?
EVER SEE A DONKEY JAM?
PLEASE DEFINE A POTHOLE
IS IT LIKE A MOUSE HOLE?
I SAW A GRAY SQUIRREL
STOP A CAR ONE TIME
FIRST, SHE CROSSED THE ROAD
THEN, SHE RAN BACK AGAIN
BACK AND FORTH, SHE NEVER
COULD MAKE UP HER MIND
SHE STOPPED A CAR THAT TIME
MOST CONGESTION
HAPPENS IN A CHEST

TANKS

TANKS ARE DIFFERENT
GOLDFISH LIVE IN FISH TANKS
SOLDERS RIDE IN TANKS
SOMETIMES RUN FROM TANKS
WE HAVE TANK TOPS
NEVER SAW A TANK BOTTOM
PROPANE TANKS
HOLD PRESSURE IN
SOMETIMES MY GRANDPA
LETS HIS PRESSURE OUT
NEVER AROUND GRANDMA
WHEN PEOPLE DRINK TOO MUCH
THEN THEY GET 'TANKED'
DRIED OUT FISH TANKS
ARE WHERE TURTLES LIVE
TANKS FOR LISTENING

PASTOR TO PASTOR

PASTURAGE: A GRASSY PLACE
FOR OLD PASTORS TO GO
A LITTLE DEAD CHURCH MOUSE
GOT BORED AND THEN PASSED
FROM THIS LIFE TO THE NEXT
GRANDMA SAID "GOOD SERMON"
TO OUR PASTOR, EVERY TIME
IS THERE ANY OTHER KIND?
WHY DOES GRANDPA
ALWAYS SNORE IN CHURCH?
IS HE JUST RESTING UP
BEFORE WAKING UP?
TWO WORDS CONFUSE ME
NARTHEX AND VESTIBULE
WHY DOESN'T PASTOR PREACH
ON BOTH OF THOSE SOMETIME?

CORN

CORN LIVES IN FLAKES
I HAVE A CORN ON MY BIG TOE
WHEN MAKING CORN CHOWDER
FIRST START WITH CORN
THEN YOU ADD THE CHOWDER
DO CORN DOGS HAVE TAILS?
DO THEY HAVE TOE NAILS?
ARE CORN DOGS EVEN DOGS?
DID YOU EVER EAT ONE?
EXPLAIN CORN ON THE COB
IS IT EVER OFF THE COB?
HOW DOES IT GET OFF?
EXPLAIN A KERNAL OF CORN
THE ARMY HAS COLONELS
WHY ARE KERNALS ON COBS?
DO EARS OF CORN LISTEN?

Bill Yeomans

BONES

BONES MAKE SKELETONS
SKELETONS LIVE IN CLOSETS
THAT'S A CLOSET SKELETON
MOST BONES ARE ALIVE
MOST DOGS BURY BONES
NEVER WHILE THEY'RE ALIVE
ALL BONES ARE BORN EQUAL
LEG BONES STAY IN LEGS
THEY HOLD PEOPLE UP
EAR BONES RESIDE INSIDE EARS
BEAUTIFUL MUSIC TO CONDUCT
LEG BONES AND EAR BONES
WALKING OR LISTENING
QUITE A MYSTERY
EXPLAIN A BONE OF CONTENTION
SHOULD WE BURY IT?

CONNECTIONS

IMPORTANT PEOPLE HAVE THEM
AT LEAST SOME THINK THEY DO
BUT TO STAY CONNECTED
IS REALLY UP TO YOU
OLD FOLKS NEED CONNECTIONS
IN ALL SORTS OF WAYS
WE NEED TO FEEL CONNECTED
THROUGHOUT OUR SENIOR DAYS
WE MAY SOUND INDEPENDENT
JUST SO YOU UNDERSTAND
IF WE FALL AND CAN'T GET UP
CONNECTIONS REALLY COUNT
WITHOUT OUR CONNECTIONS
WE'RE ALONE AT BEST
HELP US FEEL CONNECTED

SMOKING

SMOKING IS FOR SMOKERS
NEVER A GOOD CHOICE
WHY ARE SOME LADIES
CALLED 'SMOKING HOT'?
SMOKING FLAVORS BACON
MAKES IT TASTE SO GOOD
WHY IS BACON BAD FOR YOU?
WHEN DOES BAD BECOME GOOD?
GRANNY HAD A CORNCOB PIPE
HELD BETWEEN HER GUMS
OLD GRANNY NEVER SMOKED IT
SHE CALLED SMOKING 'DUMB'
SMOKING ONLY STINKS YOU UP
AND CAUSES YOU TO SMELL
SMOKING SMELLS

BIRDS

MANY BIRDS HAVE FEATHERS
NOT YARD BIRDS OR JAIL BIRDS
FEATHERS STICK TO WINGS
BIRD WINGS HAVE FEATHERS
WINGS BELONG TO BIRDS
WINGS WIGGLE AND BIRDS FLY
HELICOPTERS FLY-NO WINGS
AIRPLANES HAVE WINGS
THOSE WINGS DON'T WIGGLE
BIRDS COME IN ALL SIZES
WINGS COME IN SIZES TOO
SIZES TO FIT THE BIRDS
GOD MADE BIRDS TO FLY
MANY FLY TOGETHER, WITHOUT
BUMPING INTO EACH OTHER
WHY DON'T BIRDS BUMP?

TEETH

TEETH ARE FOR CHEWING FOOD
OR FOR BITING OFF A PIECE
I GUESS, A PIECE OF SOMETHING
BABIES NEED TO GROW UP FIRST
BEFORE THEIR TEETH COME IN
OLD FOLKS SEEM TO GROW OLD
BEFORE THEIR TEETH FALL OUT
GRANNY HAS SOME FUNNY ONES
NOT LOOKING NATURAL LIKE
SINCE THEY COME OUT AT NIGHT
SHE STILL HAS HER GUMS I THINK
SOME SHARKS LOSE THEIR TEETH
ARE OLD PEOPLE LIKE SHARKS?
BITING OFF SOME PEOPLES HEADS
IS THIS WHY THEY LOSE TEETH?

LESSONS

LESSONS ARE FOR LEARNING
LEARNING AND REMEMBERING
REMEMBER IS THE HARDEST PART
LESSONS COME FROM TEACHERS
SOME ARE GOOD, OTHERS NOT SO
HISTORY TEACHES LESSONS
OLD PEOPLE UNDERSTAND
THIS MAKES US MUCH WISER
OLDER LESSONS MAKE US WISER
IF WE APPLY EACH CAREFULLY
"I HOPE SHE LEARNED A LESSON"
IS SORT OF DOUBLE-TALK
FOR. TO LEARN ANY LESSON
IS TO BE CAREFULLY TAUGHT
LIFE IS FULL OF LESSONS
WHY NOT LEARN ONE TODAY?

Bill Yeomans

WHISKERS

SENIORS UNDERSTAND WHISKERS
EVERYBODY HAS SOME
GROWING OUT SOMEWHERE
SOME MEN SHAVE THEM OFF
SOME WOMEN PLUCK THEM OUT
I FIND AS WE GROW OLDER
NEW WHISKERS SEEM TO SPROUT
I SAW A BIG BLACK WHISKER
GROW OUT A LADIES NOSE
SHE MUST'VE BEEN FAR SIGHTED
NOT TO SPOT ONE OF THOSE
I THOUGHT TO OFFER SERVICE
TO HELP HER PLUCK IT OUT
SOME THINGS SHOULD REMAIN
AS GOD INTENDED

PUPPIES

PUPPIES ARE BABY DOGS
EVERY SENIOR NEEDS ONE
TO REMIND WHEN WE WERE
BABIES A LONG TIME PAST
ANCIENT HISTORY, REMEMBER
WHEN YOU WERE THREE
OR EVEN SIXTY-THREE
PUPPIES DO THREE THINGS
EAT AND PEE AND POO
NOT SO VERY DIFFERENT
FROM ME AND EVEN YOU
PUPPIES LOVE TO TAKE A NAP
THEY GIVE US LOTS OF JOY
TILL THEY WET ON OUR LAP
LITTLE GIRL OR LITTLE BOY?

RESTFUL

CAN YOU GET REST EMPTY?
I HAVE A RIGHT TO KNOW
WHAT IS NOT ENOUGH REST?
WHEN YOUR EYES GET PUFFY?
HOW CAN YOU CATCH A NAP?
OR A LITTLE 'SHUT-EYE'?
WHAT MAKES THEM SO
HARD TO CATCH?
ARE NAPS SLIPPERY LIKE FISH?
WHENEVERY I GET GRUMPY
I GET SENT TO TAKE A NAP
DEFINE RESTFUL IF YOU CAN
PART OF BRINGING PEACE
GRANDPA GETS HIS RESTFUL
SITTING IN HIS CHAIR AT HOME
ALL ALONE IN HIS ZONE

APRONS

APRONS ARE NEVER WORN
UNLESS MAKING A MESS
WHEN MIXING STUFF TOGETHER
MAKING AND BAKING ANYTHING
THAT TASTES CHOCOLATE
GRANDPA WEARS AN APRON
WHEN WORKING IN HIS SHOP
IT HELPS KEEP THE SAWDUST
FROM GETTING IN HIS EYES
A GOOD OLD FASHONED APRON
IS LIKE A FAITHFUL FRIEND
DO KEEP ONE CLOSE AT HAND
GRANNY LOVES HER APRON
WEARS IT ALL DAY LONG
TRADES IT FOR PAJAMAS
WHEN HER DAY IS DONE

Bill Yeomans

SCRATCHING

SCRATCHING GOES WITH ITCHING
HAPPENS ALMOST EVERY TIME
ALSO HELPS WITH THINKING
ESPECIALLY FOR OLDER MEN
GIVES MORE TIME TO THINK
LOOKING PHILOSOPHICAL
LIKE STROKING A BEARD
FOR MEN WITHOUT BEARDS
SCRATCHING HEADS IN PUBLIC
WITH PEOPLE WATCHING
ANY OTHER SCRATCH MUST WAIT
UNTIL WE ARE QUITE ALONE.
HOUND DOGS SCRATCH IN PUBLIC
REFINED MEN SELDOM DO
SCRATCHING BRINGS RELIEF
THAT'S ALL I HAVE TO SAY

Attention Seniors

CLOTHES LINES

IF WE ARE REALLY OLD
WE REMEMBER CLOTHES LINES
FROM MANY YEARS AGO
BEFORE DRYERS WERE INVENTED
FIRST YOU WASHED CHOTHES
THEN YOU RINSED THEM
AND WRUNG THEM OUT
(SQUEEZED OUT THE WATER)
PILED INTO A CLOTIIES BASKET
TOOK THEM OUTSIDE AND
HUNG THEM UP TO DRY
ON A CLOTHES LINE
ATTACHED WITH CLOTHES PINS
EITHER STRAIGHT ONES
OR THE PINCHY KIND
WITH LITTLE SPRINGY THINGS

Bill Yeomans

CLOTHES LINES 2

THESE CLOTHES LINES WERE
FASTENED FROM BUILDINGS OR
TREES AND STRETCHED OUT
PRETTY FAR AND SAGGED.
A FORKED STICK WAS USED
TO PROP THEM UP, SORT OF TO
HELP TAKE OUT THE SLACK.
DOES THIS BRING MEMORIES?
REMEMBER THE PULLIES? OR NOT
LADIES UNDIES KEPT HIDDEN
FROM NEIGHBORS PRYING EYES
COULDN'T HAVE NEIGHBORS
GUESSING WHAT SIZE
OR HOW MUCH LACE
OR KNOWING FOR SURE
WHAT YOU WORE UNDER

PUDDLES

LADIES AVOIDED PUDDLES
WEARING OPEN TOED SHOES
SHOES WITH HOLES UP FRONT
TO LET THE TOES STICK OUT
PUDDLES ARE LARGE HOLES
FOR MUDDY WATER
AFTER THE RAINS COME
MY FRIEND HAD A DOG
HER NAME WAS 'PUDDLES'
DIFFERENT KIND OF PUDDLE
SOME PUDDLES GROW UP
AND BECOME LITTLE PONDS
SOME PUDDLES DRY UP
AND JUST BECOME MUD
LADIES TAKE MUD BATHS
DON'T KNOW WHY

Bill Yeomans

MEMORY

ITS HARD TO REMEMBER
WHEN I LAST HAD A MEMORY
I HEARD IT HAD ESCAPED ME
WHY WOULD IT WANT TO?
I CANNOT UNDERSTAND WHY
IT WOULD WANT TO LEAVE
WAS IT CROWDED OUT
NO LONGER ANY ROOM
WAS IT A PRIVATE ROOM?
MAYBE ROOM TO IMPROVE?
IS MY MEMORY LOST AND GONE?
DID YOU REMEMBER YOURS?
WHAT IT LOOKED LIKE
IS IT REALLY OLD?
LOST BUT NOT FORGOTTEN?
I WONDER

PAPERWORK

DOES PAPER REALLY WORK?
IF NOT – WHY NOT?
NOBODY LIKES PAPERWORK
IT MAKES YOUR FINGERS SWEAT
THEN PAPER GETS STICKY
PAPERWORK DOESN'T WORK
WHEN IT GETS ALL WET
WET PAPERWORK GETS SMUDGES
PEOPLE DON'T READ SMUDGES
PAPERWORK HURTS EYES AND
CONNECTS TO OUR BRAIN
PAPERWORK HURTS YOUR BRAIN
WHY HURT YOUR BRAIN?
MUCH BETTER IDEA TO
FORGET PAPERWORK
FOREVER

TEMPTATIONS

TEMPTATIONS ARE WRONG
BUT THEY ARE SO TEMPTING
OFTEN HARD TO RESIST
PROCRASTINATION IS ONE
I PUT THINGS OFF AT TIMES
AT TIMES I TAKE THINGS OFF
DO YOU EVER FEEL TEMPTED?
DON'T CARE, JUST ASKING
TRYING TO BE POLITE
CAN'T STAND TEMPTATIONS
LIKE ADAM AND EVE
SO VERY TEMPTING
WOULD ANYBODY KNOW
SUCH A DELICIOUS APPLE
TEMPTATION WAS THERE
JUST TO TAKE A BITE

MENDING

MENDING IS AN ART FORM
IT TAKES ALL SHAPES AND SIZES
A NEEDLE AND THREAD WITH
WILLING HANDS CAN MEND
TORN CLOTH, TORN RELATIONS
MENDING FENCES ALSO WORKS
MENDING IS REPAIRING THINGS
STRONGER AND BETTER
LIKE BUILDING RELATIONSHIPS
UPON A STRONG FOUNDATION
BROKEN REMAINS BROKEN
MENDING FIXES BROKEN
DO YOU KNOW A 'BROKEN'?
MENDING IS AN ART FORM
MENDING REPAIRS BROKEN

Bill Yeomans

LONELY

OLD FOLKS MAY FEEL LONELY
WHEN LIVING ALL ALONE
OTHERS MAY FEEL LONELY
WITH PEOPLE ALL AROUND
WHEN WE FEEL DISCONNECTED
IS WHEN LONLINESS SETS IN
KNOW SOMEONE WHO IS LONELY
GIVE HER A FRIENDLY CALL
FRIENDLINESS BEATS LONELY
IF WE PRACTICE FRIENDLY
WE DRIVE LONELY AWAY
LONELY BOTHERS EVERYONE
ONE WAY OR ANOTHER
WE CAN BEAT OLD LONELY
BE A GOOD SISTER
OR A BROTHER

WONDERING

WHEN WE GET TO 'OLDER'
IS WHERE WONDERING BEGINS
ASKING COUNTLESS QUESTIONS
WITH SOME INVOLVING SIN
WONDERING WHO MADE US
HOW IT ALL BEGAN
IS GOD THE CREATOR
PART OF HIS PERFECT PLAN
WONDERING IS NATURAL
HOW WE'RE MADE TO BE
IS GETTING OLD PART OF AGEING?
I WAS JUST WONDERING
HOW THIS "OLD" WORKS
HOW HUMMINGBIRDS
AND BUMBLE BEES ARE NOT
SUPPOSED TO FLY

Bill Yeomans

BUTTONS

BUTTONS WERE CREATED
TO FIT BUTTONHOLES
SOMEWHAT LIKE A PIDGEONHOLE
MADE FOR HIDING THINGS
BUTTONHOLES COULD HIDE
BELLY-BUTTONS OR NAVALS
BUTTONHOLES HOLD BUTTONS
GRANDMA SAID FOR ME TO
"BUTTON YOUR LIP"
HOW IS IT POSSIBLE?
A LIP BUTTONHOLE?
BUTTONS NEED ATTACHMENT
WITH THREAD OR SAFETY PINS
SAFETY PINS SHOULD WORK
DON'T YOU THINK?
TELL ME IF I'M WRONG

VERTICAL

VERTICAL MEANS UPRIGHT
MOSTLY AS IN STANDING UP
STRAIGHT AS A BOARD
I'VE SEEN WARPED BOARDS
DOES UPRIGHT MAKE WARPED?
CAN VERTICAL DO THIS?
STANDING IMPLIES VERTICAL
AFTER STRETCHING OUT
TO OUR FULL POTENTIAL
IS SLEEPING 'UN-VERTICAL'?
LIKE REVERSING VERTICAL
PUTTING IT TO BED AT NIGHT
DOES VERTICAL EVER SLEEP?
HORIZONTAL IS KINDER
SHE'S SMARTER TOO
KNOWS HOW TO TAKE A NAP

Bill Yeomans

IN BETWEEN

IN BETWEEN BREAKFAST
CAUSES HUNGER PAINS
IN BETWEEN THE COVERS
IS MY GREATEST DELIGHT
TO TUCK MYSELF UNDER
ON A COLD, FROSTY NIGHT
IN BETWEEN SENTENCES
TENDS TO BE FORGETFUL
IN BETWEEN THE CUSHIONS
SO THAT I CAN'T SEE
IS MY SET OF CAR-KEYS
HIDING THERE FROM ME
TWEEN A ROCK AND HARD PLACE
IS NOT A GOOD PLACE TO BE
BETWEEN TWO FRIENDS WHO
LOVE YOU, IS LIVING HAPPILY

PILL TAKERS

PILL MAKERS LOVE PILL TAKERS
ITS AN UNDISPUTED FACT
THE MORE WE TAKE
THE MORE THEY MAKE
PILL TAKERS ARE WONDERFUL
WE'RE EVEN PREDICTABLE
WE OBEY OUR DOCTORS ORDERS
WRITTEN ON THE BOTTLE
IN LITTLE TINY LETTERS
THAT OLD FOLKS CANNOT SEE
IF YOU CANNOT READ THE LABEL
YOU TAKE PILLS ANYTIME
WHENEVER YOU REMEMBER
I HOPE YOU'RE FEELING FINE
PILL TAKERS BECOME SHAKERS
CHILD-PROOF BOTTLES ROCK

Bill Yeomans

HALLS

HALLS HAVE LONG WALLS
WITH TOPS AND BOTTOMS
SENIORS WALK ON BOTTOMS
BOTTOMS OF THE HALLS
OLD PEOPLE HAVE BOTTOMS
SOME HAVE BLOWN THEIR TOPS
ALL THOSE TOPS HAVE GONE
SOME HALLS HAVE DOORS
AND WINDOWS OF OPPORTUNITY
MOST HALLS LEAD PLACES
EXPLAIN HALLS OF CONGRESS
WHERE OLD PEOPLE GO TO DIE?
HALLS OFFER US DIRECTIONS
WE CHOOSE WHERE TO GO
WE HAVE DESTINATIONS
HALLS JUST GO, AND GO, AND GO

SHIFTING

SHIFTING GEARS MENT KNOWING
HOW TO USE A CLUTCH
OR WHEN TO USE A CLUTCH
OR WHAT A CLUTCH WAS
SHIFTING IS TO CHANGE SPEED
OR SHIFTING YOUR POSITION
TURNING OVER AT NIGHT
OLD PEOPLE SHIFT THE BLAME
FOR THEIR FORGETTING LIKE
"I MUST BE GETTING OLDER"
COURSE YOU'RE GETTING OLDER
NOBODYS GETTING YOUNGER
SOME SHIFT FROM FOOT TO FOOT
TO GIVE EACH ONE A REST
SHIFTING BACK AND FORTH

FOLLOWING

FOLLOWING IS NOT LEADING
ASK A FOUR HORSE TEAM
MOST OLD FOLKS REMEMBER
ORIGINAL HORSEPOWER
WHEN HORSES PULLED THINGS
WITH A FOUR HORSE TEAM
TWO WERE LEADERS IN FRONT
THEY ALWAYS GOT TO SEE
THE OTHER TWO, FOLLOWING
THINK WHAT THEY HAD TO SEE
FOLLOWING GOOD ADVICE
IS EASY, WE ALL AGREE
BUT THE HORSE WHO IS LEADER
SEES OPPORTUNITY
FOLLOW YOUR DREAM

DREAMS

DREAMS ARE SOMETIMES VISIONS
VISIONS COME IN DREAMS
OLD PEOPLE HAVE DAYDREAMS
SOME HAVE PIPE DREAMS
DREAMS ARE EXPECTATIONS
OF BETTER THINGS TO COME
WHEN WE GO TO SLEEP
WE DREAM WE'LL HAVE ONE
HOW DO DREAMS START?
WHERE DO THEY FINISH?
AT TIMES GOD USES DREAMS
TO SPEAK HIS WORDS TO US
AND OFFER UNDERSTANDING
TO GIVE A LOVING TOUCH
HE LOVES US SO MUCH

Bill Yeomans

PROCRASTINATION

THE ART OF PROCRASTINATION
COUSIN TO HESITATION
FRIEND OF CONSTERNATION
AVOIDS PERSPIRATION
DISAVOWS ORGANIZATION
HATES PREPERATION
LOOKS AT OBSERVATION
AVOIDS REPOPULATION
PERFORMS AMPUTATION
DESTROYS COOPERATION
ENCOURAGES PERPETUATION
DIVIDES MULTIPLICATION
LOVES PONTIFICATION
ADORES JUSTIFICATION
PROCRASTINATION
LOVES PROCRASTINATORS

LIFTING

"SHE NEVER LIFTS A FINGER
TO HELP IN ANY WAY"
THAT'S A QUOTE AN OLD GUY
SWEARS, HE HEARD GRANNY SAY.
SWEARING IS NEVER COOL BUT
ANYONE CAN LIFT A FINGER
ESPECIALLY A LITTLE 'PINKY'
ELDERS DON'T LIKE LIFTING
SEEMS TO HURT THE BACK
AND THE HIPS, AND THE KNEES
ARCHES AND THE ANKLES HURT
LIFTING IS NOT A BREEZE
LIFTING OFTEN DEFIES GRAVITY
IF YOU ATTEMPT A LIFTING
GOD HELP YOU IF YOU SNEEZE

PERSONALITY

WE ALL HAVE PERSONALITY
SOME TRY TO HIDE IT, OTHERS
LET IT ALL HANG OUT
DEFINED BY PERSONALITY
EACH ONE HAS HER OWN
HAPPY IS ONE CHARACTER
ANOTHER WEARS HER FROWN
SOME DEFINED AS PERSONABLE
NOT SURE WHAT THAT COULD BE
A DESCRIPTIVE ADJECTIVE
FOR EVERYONE TO SEE
A REAL FINE PERSONALITY
IS SOMETHING TO BEHOLD
COMPLAINING HAS NO PLACE
WHEN WE ENJOY GROWING OLD

LAWYERS

MOST LAWYERS PRACTICE LAW
WHY DO THEY NEED PRACTICE?
LAWYERS PRODUCE TRUSTS
DOES ANYONE TRUST LAWYERS?
TRUST EQUALS SECURITY
THAT MEANS FEELING SAFE
GRANDPA HAS THIS SAYING
"LAWYERS SWIM WITH SHARKS"
CAN ALL LAWYERS SWIM?
OR DO SHARKS WALK ON LAND?
LAWYERS ARE CONFUSING
WHAT IS A LOAN SHARK?
ANOTHER KIND OF LAWYER?
ALL SHARKS HAVE BIG TEETH
SOME ARE LABELED 'ESQUIRE'
THOSE ARE THE LAWYERS

Bill Yeomans

FREEZING

SENIORS HAVE THINNING BLOOD
THAT'S WHAT MAKES US COLD
AS FAR AS I'VE BEEN TOLD
FREEZING IS DEEPER COLD
WHAT CAUSES SHIVERING
FREEZING MAKES ME BONE COLD
AS COLD AS COLD CAN BE
FREEZING IS GOOD EXERCISE
IT LUBRICATES THE PARTS
AND GETS THE FEET TO MOVING
BEFORE THE FREEZING STARTS
FREEZING IS AN ADJECTIVE
WHICH CAN BECOME A VERB
FOR FREEZING SOMEONE OUT
I THINK THAT IS ABSURD
ICE CREAM IS GOOD FREEZING

MORE FREEZING

IF MAN DISCOVERED FREEZING
LADIES INVENTED COATS
ANIMALS ARE BORN WITH COATS
OF MANY SHAPES AND SIZES
POLAR BEARS AND POLAR COATS
NOT ONE EVER FREEZING
FREEZING IS WHEN MOLECULES
LEARN TO TRAVEL SLOW
FREEZING IS WHEN SENIORS
TURN BLUE IN THE SNOW
DON'T MAKE FUN OF SENIORS
SOME DAY YOU MAY BE ONE
UNDERSTANDING FREEZING
WHILE SITTING IN THE SUN
MAKING OLD BONES RATTLE
UNTIL THE FREEZINGS DONE

SOMEDAY – ONE DAY

SOMEDAY BECOMES ONE DAY
IF CHORES ARE NEEDING DONE
OLD MEN CLAIMING SOMEDAY
"I'LL GET AROUND TO THAT"
ALL THE TIME FORGETTING
WHERE HIS 'THAT' IS AT
LADIES HOPE THAT ONE DAY
WHEN ALL THE WORK IS DONE
THEY WILL FEEL THE FREEDOM
TO GO OUT AND HAVE SOME FUN
NEVER WAIT FOR SOMEDAY
SOMEDAY MAY NEVER COME
SENIORS LIVE WITH ONE DAY
LIVE ONE DAY AT A TIME
FORGET ABOUT OLD SOMEDAY
ONE DAY IS JUST FINE

GETTING SETTLED

GRAVITY HELPS THINGS SETTLE
GETTING SETTLED IS SAGGING
ANOTHER WORD FOR SETTLING
LIKE GETTING BOGGED DOWN
SETTLED INTO A NEW JOB
OR SETTLED INTO A ROUTINE
YOU MIGHT GET UNSETTLED
WHEN THINGS GO HAYWIRE
WHAT DOES HAYWIRE MEAN?
PLEASE TELL ME IF YOU KNOW
WRITE ME A LETTER
I NEED TO GET IT SETTLED
COULD GETTING SETTLED MEAN
LETTING GRAVITY REIN FREE?
WITH NO RESTRICTIONS EVER
WHAT WILL BE, WILL BE?

Bill Yeomans

LOSING IT

PLEASE HELP DESCRIBE AN 'IT'
HOW TO KNOW I'M LOSING 'IT'
CAN'T START LOOKING FOR 'IT'
WITHOUT KNOWING 'IT'
OR EVEN UNDERSTANDING 'IT'
IS 'IT' LOST OR GETTING LOST?
WHAT IF I FIND 'IT'?
WILL I RECOGNIZE 'IT'?
EXACTLY WHO IS LOSING 'IT'?
CAN YOU LOSE 'IT' TWO TIMES?
CAN OTHERS FIND 'IT' FOR YOU?
IS LOSING 'IT' DIFFICULT?
IF AND WHEN YOU FIND 'IT'
WILL 'IT' EVER SEEM THE SAME?
IS 'IT' WARM AND FUZZY?
I THINK I'M LOSING 'IT'

SCALES

NOT ALL FISH HAVE SCALES
SOME ARE MADE WITH SKIN
OLD FOLKS GET SCALY SKIN
SCALY SKIN CAN GO AWAY
DIFFERENT FROM FISH ONES
SCALES ARE FOR TELLING
HOW LITTLE-MUCH YOU WEIGH
LIKE THE SCALES OF JUSTICE
FOR WEIGHING HONESTY
WHAT HAPPENS TO TIP SCALES?
DO THEY TIP WAY OVER?
CAN THEY GET STRAIGHT AGAIN?
FISH SCALES ARE SLIPPERY
FOR SLIPPING THROUGH WATER
SCALES OFFER PROTECTION
FROM MANY NASTY THINGS

Bill Yeomans

__STRETCHING__

STRETCHING STRETCHES YOU
IN MANY DIFFERENT WAYS
STRETCHING THE TRUTH ISN'T
REALLY STRETCHING AT ALL
THAT IS FLAT OUT WRONG
THAT KIND WILL SNAP AT YOU
BODY STRETCHING IS GOOD
STRETCHING MAKES US LONGER
STRETCHING HELPS SENIORS
REMEMBER WHERE THINGS ARE
AND HOW WE'RE ATTACHED
IT LOOSENS VERTEBRAE
HELPS THE BACK TO POP
STRETCHING NEVER HURTS US
KEEPS US FEELING FIT
FIT AS A FIDDLE?

BENDING

BENDING MEANS GETTING BENT
NOT "BENT OUT OF SHAPE"
NOT A GOOD KIND OF BENDING
BENDING PREVENTS BREAKING
LIKE PALM TREES IN THE WIND
LEARN TO BEND A LITTLE
AND EVERYBODY WINS
BENDING IS FORGIVING
IN EVERY SINGLE WAY
BENDING HELPS WE SENIORS
ENDURE THROUGH EVERY DAY
BENDING HELPS US PHYSICALLY
WHEN WE ENDURE PAIN
BENDING HELPS OUR BLOOD
FLOW BACK TO OUR BRAIN
BENDING BUILDS BRAIN POWER!

Bill Yeomans

WINDOWS

WINDOWS ARE FOR LOOKING OUT
SOMETIMES LOOKING IN
OR FOR LOOKING INWARD
LIKE A WINDOW INTO THE SOUL
WINDOWS LET THE SUNLIGHT IN
KEEP THE SHADOWS OUT
SOME COVER THEM WITH SHADES
TO KEEP THE SUNLIGHT OUT
WINDSHIELDS KEEP 'WINDY'
FROM GETTING IN YOUR HAIR
WINDSHIELDS ARE FOR SEEING
NEED CONSTANT CLEANING TO
REMOVE DEAD BUGS AND GUTS
DRIVE ALONG AND THEN 'SPLAT'!
SHE DIDN'T DESERVE THAT
ONE OF GOD'S CREATURES

TIME TWO

TIME WAS INVENTED BY WOMEN
TO HOLD MEN IN CHECK
GOD CREATED EVERYTHING ELSE
TIME IS A HUMAN CREATION
WE TOOK DAY AND NIGHT
AND WERE NOT SATISFIED
IT'S FINE FOR ALL CREATION
SUN AND MOON WORKED FINE
ALL THE ANIMAL KINGDOM
HAS NEVER NEEDED TIME
I FIND AS I GET OLDER
TIME SEEMS TO SIMPLY FLY
DON'T KNOW WHERE IT ENDED UP
AND I CHOOSE TO NOT ASK WHY
TIME GIVES US ANXIETY, SO I'M
CONTENT TO LET IT FLY

SINGING

SINGING IS A GIFT OF GOD
I TRULY LOVE TO SING OUT
HOWEVER, AS THE YEARS GO BY
MY SONG BECOMES A SHOUT
VOCAL CHORDS LOSE 'VOCAL'
AND TONE JUST FLYS AWAY
MATTERS NOT HOW MUCH I TRY
SOUNDS LIKE A DONKEY'S BRAY
'PLEASE SING SOFTER' IS TO SAY
'DO YOUR SINGING FAR AWAY'
I MAY BE GETTING OLDER
AND SINGING AIN'T SO SWEET
SINGING IS FROM IN, NOT OUT
THE WAY THAT IT SHOULD BE
SINGING KEEPS ME HAPPY

CLEANING

CLEANING OPPOSES DIRTYING
AND MESSING THINGS ALL UP
CLEANING INVOLVES BRUSHING
NO REASON FOR BRUSHING
ANYTHING EXCEPT TEETH
OR MAYBE LADIES' HAIR
NO NEED TO DO MUCH CLEANING
IT NEVER STAYS THAT WAY
CLEANING INVOLVES WASHING
WASHING HAS SOME MERIT
WASH FACE AND BODY PARTS
STAY CLEAN INSIDE AND OUT
YOUR INSIDE IS IMPORTANT
WHY WASH FLOORS SINCE
NO ONE COMES KNOCKING
FLOORS ARE FOR WALKING

WORRY

WORRY IS FOR WORRY WARTS
WHATEVER THOSE THINGS ARE
WORRY CAUSES WORRY LINES
SOME MIGHT CALL A FROWN
TO WORRY AIN'T DEPENDING
ON GOD FOR MOST ANYTHING
AS FAR AS I REMEMBER
WORRY NEVER EARNED A DIME
'WORRY IS AS WORRY DOES'
THAT SOUNDS PRETTY 'CATCHY'
WORRY MAY CAUSE ULCERS
OR OTHER BELLY ACHES
WORRY CAN EVEN MAKE YOU ILL
THIS CAN CAUSE YOU WORRY
WHO INVENTED WORRY?

ENDING

ENDING IS A BRIEF PAUSE
BEFORE WE START AGAIN
LIKE THE END OF A RACE
SORT OF LIKE FINISHING
BUT NOT QUITE
I BELIEVE THAT I'M READY
TO END THIS SILLY BOOK
HOPE YOU HAD A CHUCKLE
OR MAYBE EVEN TWO
PERHAPS I'LL WRITE ANOTHER
BEFORE THIS LIFE IS THROUGH
IT'S BEEN A 'KICK'
TO SAY THE LEAST
AS MUCH FUN FOR YOU
AS IT WAS FOR ME?
GOD BLESS YOU ALL

Books by this Author

Power Verses - To Strengthen Your Walk

The Face of God - Reflected in Nature

Christ Centered Marriage

Christ Centered Finances

Christ Centered Families

Bill I Am - An Autobiography

My Heart Made New A Personal Testimony

Spirit Power - Holy Spirit Throughout History

Attention SENIORS - Life's a Chuckle

Available on AMAZON

Made in the USA
Columbia, SC
11 September 2018